Transparent As Always

Tiara Smith

BookLeaf
Publishing

India | USA | UK

Presentation by *BookLeaf Publishing*

Web: www.bookleafpub.com

E-mail: info@bookleafpub.com

ISBN: 9789357214711

First edition 2022

Dedicated to Papa Julius, Kai, the man with the mirror, and all of the "Sunshiny people."

ACKNOWLEDGEMENT

Before he passed, my "Papa" always encouraged me to be my most authentic self. I live freely every day in his honor. This acknowledgment page is dedicated solely to him. He has positively impacted so many lives, and I am reminded of this twice a year: on his birthday and the anniversary of his death. I love when people mourn him with me and share their memories. Thank you for being my light.

PREFACE

I planned to organize this by subject or emotion, but I decided not to. I wanted it to feel as jumbled and disorganized as I do at times.

Excerpt from "Tell Me About Yourself" by Tiara Allure

When someone says, "tell me about yourself", I never know what to say or I know exactly what I want to say, but it comes out wrong or jumbled. My mind instantly races with all of these wonderful qualities that I love about myself, but I think my mind moves faster than my mouth and my tongue just cannot keep up. By the time the words travel from my Broca's area to my motor cortex and out of my mouth, it sounds like gibberish. After that, I settle for saying something boring like, "I like art." Or "Pink is my favorite color!" I think it is the excitement of talking about myself, but it also happens when I talk about other subjects that I am interested in. Whatever it is, it needs to stop. You know what else needs to stop? That gap between someone saying something to me and the time it takes for me to respond because I have so much going on in my head that I have yet to process what they said, and, in a quick effort to respond, I say something basic and spacy. Now I look dumb. My goodness. Excuse my quick stream of consciousness, but this is how my mind works on a daily basis. Oh my, is this why I tend to

switch the topic several times during a
conversation? I have the attention span of a
puppy and so many interesting subjects
bouncing around in my mind. So please be kind.

The Unpicked Flower

Imagine what could happen if you weren't afraid
to touch me.
Is it possible that our alliance could set us free?
If I am the flower, would that make you the bee?

I think we would be symbiotic.
If you pollinate me, I'll give you my nectar,
And everyone could benefit from our union.
Let's develop a love that angers the soul
collector,
And build a bond that no one can ruin.

You can be my protector;
Nothing too chaotic.
Life can write our story.
Though it may (hopefully) be erotic,
I wouldn't put it in that category.

Label it as another kind of romance;
I wish that we could hold hands.
But, We don't have them.
That is the excuse that keeps us at opposing
ends.
I have petals and stems;
You have wings and eyes that shine like gems...

I wish you weren't afraid.
You've already invaded my heart.
Together we would be like art.

But, you say that I am a flower,
So delicate and beautiful, I shouldn't be picked.

If you are the bee, and I am the flower,
 will you leave me here for another man to
devour?

The Sweetest Cupcake in the Bakery

I can be addictive like a narcotic
 and put you to sleep like one too.
Place you in a trance; I am hypnotic.
 Listen to my voice and watch how I move.
I'll will you into a love so chaotic,
 You wouldn't know what to do.
I may be a little psychotic,
but I can tell, so are you.

Less Sugar, More Water

Less sugar, more water.
Go harder, go harder.
How do you expect to succeed
If you don't push yourself til you bleed?
How do you expect to be happy when your hair
is so nappy?
And your skin is so dark? Life isn't a walk in the
park.
You must assimilate to be great.

You have something to say? It can wait.
Don't speak your mind; we don't care.
And let's get back to this hair.
Surely you plan to relax it?
You are beautiful, I'll admit.
But your ego, you should deflate.

I'm not trying to berate
But, I mean, who are you?
No one. You are no one.
You are a face.
You are a body.
Your confidence is so out of place.
How do you expect to date?

I said do not speak. Wait.
Be less vocal.
Be more humble.
Be more foreign; you look too local.
Think less.
Smile more.
You have opinions? Such a bore.
Do not even express that you're irate.

Yes, this is a date.
You don't understand? What don't you get?
I asked you out, but I didn't plan to pay for it.
Gold digger. Ask for the bill; we'll split.
You have standards... as a woman? That's a toxic
trait.

And I see you've been gaining weight.
Women should be thick, but not too thick.
Be thin.
How do you expect to win without a husband?
Don't you want to be a wife?
What do you mean there is more to life?
Goals? Money causes marital strife.
Clean the home and be quiet.
Shush. Please do not prate.

You are such an ingrate.
My advice is simple:
Consume less sugar.

Drink more water.
Eat less.
Speak Less.
Think Less.
Be Less.

Be Less.

The Man in the Mirror

Have you ever felt like something was off, but you couldn't quite put your finger on it? I've felt "off" for a while now, and though I've been able to connect a few of the pieces, it took meeting this man for me to put the puzzle together. In the beginning, the man came to me with gifts. He spoke words that I so desperately needed to hear. Not the deceptive ones that are pleasing to the ear. Unaware of how they were affecting me. Unaware that he'd appeared in the middle of my healing. Unaware that he'd turn a facade into a reality.

A few weeks ago, he stopped coming with his usual gifts. Instead, he brought a mirror. This wasn't like the mirror that hangs in my shower; it wasn't there to validate me. When I looked into the mirror, I saw, not who I am, but who I was becoming. Dark.

I started to become everything that I'd despised before: Vengeful, deceitful, manipulative, and opportunistic. When I realized this, I began to make excuses for my evil, but that didn't make it any less evil. Especially not, when in God's eyes, all sins are equal. Now that I recognize what was forming within me, I could not, in good conscience, allow myself to proceed.

I know what it feels like to be used and taken advantage of, and I refuse to continue to inflict that pain upon others. Not for power. Not for greed. Even if I feel like they deserve it. He that is without sin cast the first stone. I'm not perfect. Who am I to judge? This man came like light and pulled me out of the dark. As I glanced at my reflection, I began to self-reflect. "What brought me to this point?"

So, I've ended my villain arc. Once a prisoner to my trauma, now I am freed. This man, his gifts, and his mirror saved me.

At least, Not Today

Sometimes I can't bring myself to speak.
I can't smile or wave or say "have a great day!"
I feel weak.

If I'm a giver, who can't give, what does that
make me?
I used to feel inadequate when I couldn't give
impart my energy.
I decided to release myself from that mentality.

Today, I don't feel happy and that's okay.
I'm not going to fake it, not today.
I'm not going to force myself to show up;
I simply cannot make it.

I'm giving myself space to breathe,
And time to grieve;
Permission to be angry.

I can't be strong all of the time,
Or happy all of the time,
Or even ardent all of the time.

I need a moment to feel.
I need time to heal.

I don't feel happy, and I won't pretend.
I've got way too many wounds to mend.

I can't put a smile on.
I just can't fake it; at least, not today.
Today, they're going to have to see me naked.

I'm human.
I'm healing.
I refuse to be sorry for how I am feeling.

At least for today.

Dear Heavenly Father

I know it's been a while. I really don't know
what to say.
I'm not even exactly sure how to pray.
Am I doing it right?
I'm afraid that I might mess it up, and you'll be
on your way.
Hopefully, it won't be tonight.
Life got dark, and I know you're the only reason
I made it through.
So, If you can hear me, I just wanted to say
thank you.

Magnitude

When HE went away, I spiraled.
I felt like a leg had been cut off of my table, I
lost my balance,
 and I was unable to stand alone.
I was spinning, and people were talking; the
only voice I could hear was my own.

"Danger! Warning! We are in uncharted
territory! We cannot do this!" I was thrown.

 I decided to reconnect with my demons and
devour the men who approached me. I
flourished in the light of the attention; I reveled
in power stolen from a man I'd broken. But… I
was still spiraling. Manic, like he was at a point.
I'd panic.

"What am I going to do with this kid? What am I
going to do with my life?" You wouldn't believe
what I almost did.

 I felt empty, but my heart was heavy, and my
pain was constant. I isolated myself. I fell into
darkness. Either the people stopped talking, or I
stopped noticing. But I didn't mind it. I found

peace in the silence. I rediscovered God in the
solitude. He spoke to me. He said, "Do this, and
go here."

Someone was waiting at every destination.

I Gave Birth to Love

I gave birth to love and watched it grow.
 Like a flower, I watched it bloom.
I remember that day so vividly; it was the first
snow.
 Now it's sprinting across the room.

I gave birth to love and named it "sea,"
 because that is where I feel free.
I gave birth to dreams.
 Now they have come to fruition.
I gave birth to my recovery,
 and started strengthening my intuition.

You're the shell that came out of me,
 but you helped me come out of mine.
I was worried who you'd grow to be,
 but, so far, you've turned out fine.

I gave birth to a warrior, and a willow tree,
 And a pure heart who will lead me to victory.
I gave birth to you, but you restored me.

Value of Self

I believe that you have to know who you are. If you do not, it leaves room for people to try and tell you who you are. If you want to be confused, you can listen to them. I don't need anyone to tell me who I am. I know who I am.

I value self. Self-reflection, self-awareness, self-accountabilty.
I often ask myself, "Who am I becoming, and why?"
So, who am I? I do not need anyone to tell me.

I am Tiara Allure.
I am that smart, weird girl whose heart used to be pure.
I make a man question if he has an ego.
I am the villain, and the neighborhood hero.
I am a threat, but I am not threatening.
I am who I am, but I am not who they say I am.

Ind

As my body heals from the damage you've
caused, so does my mind. In a few more years,
I'll have left you behind. Unless I still love you,
then I'll be in a bind.
Surely the world would not be that unkind.

I Don't Hate You

I'm trying to remember the moment we started hating each other. It's like one day we woke up, and our demons didn't play well together anymore.

I don't even think I hate you.

I hate how you made me feel, wondering if it was ever real.
I hate thinking about you, and all of the things we used to do.
I hate that you hurt me and made me feel unworthy.
I hate that we don't get along; we just argue, going back and forth like ping pong.
I hate that I don't hate you, and I hate that I want to.
I hate that you made me say "hate" so many times.
I hate that I filled this with so many rhymes.
I hate that we have so many memories, and I can't forget.
I hate that I might not be over you yet.
I hate that I don't know what to do.

I hate that you've made me hate so many things...

but I don't hate you.

Before the Storm

Have you ever noticed that it gets quiet right before a storm? Almost silent. If you aren't careful, you might mistake the quietness for peace, but it's really a warning. Something is coming.

Will you be prepared? I'm not sure, but there's no use in hiding anymore. Whatever it is, it knows where you reside. If it's not important, put it to the side, and brace yourself for the ride.

Just A Reminder

Allow yourself to feel and heal at your own pace.

I am

Focused. I set a goal and reap the reward.
Faithful. I know who I can trust.
Fearless. I'm protected by the Spirit's sword.
Tenacious. I reassess and adjust.

Yes, I Have an Ego

I was told that I'm "real quick" to toot my own horn, and I am. I've been told that I "hype" myself too much. And I do. Honestly, I don't. I don't believe you can love yourself or compliment yourself too much. Some people are afraid to speak highly of themselves for fear of coming off as conceded. Me? I'm going to give myself my flowers. I deserve them.

Do you know what I've been through? And I look like this? Yes, I have an ego.
"Have you seen me?" That's my favorite rhetorical question to ask. RHETORICAL. I don't need to be validated. I'm not a car. I remember when I looked at life and didn't think I would make it this far.

Yes, I have an ego. I am beautiful, but my love for myself is deeper than skin. When I say I love myself, the outside is included, but I'm talking about what resides within. I'm not afraid of failures; they set me up for the wins. So if I need to, I'll fail again and again.

Siren

No wonder the rush of power felt so good. You made me feel so low for so long. When I finally broke free from you, my mind couldn't comprehend the freedom. I had a breakdown. Then, I realized I had a power. I could influence anyone to do anything I wished, and, finally, I was in charge. After years of not having a voice, it came back louder and more commanding. It also came back seductive, like a siren. In two ways. Like a siren, loud and jarring. But also like a siren: Seductive. Alluring and destructive.

I'd found my voice. Well, maybe not my voice. But a voice that found me and set me free from the shackles of submission. Tira. Tina. One or the other. A combination of both. I don't know, but I know I felt powerful. It was my new addiction. I also felt guilty, "this isn't me", but my need to regain control over my life was more prominent than my desire to love thy neighbor.

I do not value the attention of men, but I capture it so effortlessly. I give them three warnings, then a grin. After that, they become an opportunity.

"Tiara, what do you need?"

"To heal."

"Too simple. Think bigger."

I have a beautiful face and a nice figure. It was never hard to pull me a nig... nice man. Well, his personality may not have been nice, but his wallet was.

I didn't even want the money. I'm a giver at heart. All of that money went to people, portfolios, and art. See, I'm generous and smart. I just wanted the feeling of being heard. It was how I got my needs met. Years of neglect and making myself small. Now I'm tall, now I'm vocal, now I'm... A siren.

If I am being honest, I wasn't consciously doing it at first, luring men off the edge. It just happened. But, at some point, I woke up in a puddle of blood, surrounded by dead bodies. It was already too late. I was already addicted. I was thriving. I was surviving. I was...

A siren.

The Sunshiny People

There is something to be said about people who,
in the middle of their darkness, choose to be a
light for others.
They are always speaking positively, and they
spread joy to all they encounter.
The people who you've probably never seen
without a smile.
You've never seen them cry, so you assume it
has been a while.
These are the sunshiny people.
They fight their demons in private, they carry
their burdens in silence, and they make sure not
to let their fires burn you.

If they can't stand tall, then they might not speak
at all.
When it becomes too much, they isolate.
They sit in solitude, not to be rude, but to protect
those around them.
They are selfless; they don't want to spread
negativity.

They hide their tears and mute their screams.
When you speak, their smile beams.
Though these people emit a light,

Their life is not as bright as it seems.

-A Stream of Consciousness-

It's been eight years, but it still feels like
yesterday. I don't think I'll ever forget. I
remember everything leading up to the moment I
walked into the room and saw your lifeless body
in that bed. I saw my father cry. I died that day
too. It's an image that I'll never be able to get
out of my head. I miss you. I think of you often.
I see your face, but the sound of your voice has
softened. I have memories, but the voice is
distorted. I can't remember your voice. Why
can't I remember? It kills me. Now the
memories play like silent films because I'd
rather hear no voice than a voice that's not
yours. 8 years. Eight years stressed and
depressed, but still trying to progress. Pretending
to be absolutely happy when I know I've never
healed. The feelings, I've suppressed. I just want
to make you proud of me, so I do my best to live
freely. I am who you always told me to be: my
most eccentric, authentic self. Never conform to
what's considered the norm. I learned so much
from watching your ambition. You told me
women belong everywhere, not just in the
kitchen. So I set my sights on everything.   My
current goal, after the diploma, is the ring. I

want to be loved how I watched you love her.
You always smiled. So I smile too, and I hope
that I can be as influential as you. I don't mean
to get dark. I don't want to die, but sometimes
I… um, I cross my heart, and I hope to sleep
forever. Because the only place I can be with
you is in my dreams. I close my eyes, and I pray
we'll stay together. I know what it sounds like,
but it's not what it seems. I just want to say I'm
sorry, and I love you. I know you've passed, but
I wish it wasn't true. I've been lost. But Papa, I
promise I'm going to find myself. And
everything I said, I'll do.

Weight Training

I'm so tired of being called strong. I hear it far too often, "You are so strong!" I don't want to be strong; I want to be happy. I know it's meant to be a compliment, but what exactly are you complimenting? My ability to carry my burdens? My ability to carry the world on my shoulders and still make room for your burdens as well? And what about those who are "weak"? Those who aren't "strong" enough to carry the weight, so they sit it down? I wish peace to the families of the "weak". Do you even know what being strong is? Imagine you're carrying this heavy weight around daily. Then one day, the weight is less heavy. As the days pass, the weight gets lighter and lighter until it feels like nothing. Not because you've gotten rid of the weight, you've just gotten used to carrying it. Essentially, you are complimenting my ability to mask my struggles and make them look good. What about those who can't? I call it weight training. You lift this weight until it stops feeling heavy, then more weight gets added, and you repeat the cycle. Maybe I'm not consuming enough protein, but It's exhausting.

Please be careful with people, and love on your "strong" friends. Some of us are tired. Some of us are not even strong; we are just acting.

Find Me in the Silence

If I die, please don't cry. Look for me.
You can find me in the silence. That's where I
found peace.
To escape from the violence, I'd run to the trees.
They'd release, and I'd inhale.
 I'd exhale, and they'd intake.
This moment would give me the strength to
prevail;
If it didn't, I'd go to the lake.

I would sit and listen to the splash,
feeling more tranquil as the hours passed.
I found peace amongst the birds and the bugs.
I loved listening to them sing.
Serenity hit me like drugs.
I could let go of everything.

You could find me on a hike.
Nature is the perfect remedy.
My dopamine levels would spike
as the wind played a melody.

You can find me in the trees
or in the flowers with the bees.
I'll be where the animals roam.

Don't look for me in a house.
I might be in clouds,
but nature is what I called home.

So please, do not cry.
I will be here for you, Kai.
If you ever need guidance,
You can find me in the silence.